Awakening on New Years Day, 2015 before anyone else in the house, I grabbed a few books. I sat down with a cup of coffee in the front room overlooking my mother-in-law's farm. The window faced east, but in the morning light the day was proving to be gray.

My reading led me to a strange selection to start the new year. With little warning, I landed on a post-Holocaust reflection from Elie Wiesel, the Jewish professor who lived through the horrors of Auschwitz.

During his outrageous ordeal, Wiesel, along with the rest of the camp, was forced to witness a hanging. The victims consisted of two adults and a young boy. The inhumane treatment would not be tempered by a speedy death for the boy as his light body weight meant it took longer for him to die. Reading, I felt myself wince. I turned my head slightly as if I could somehow deflect the full force of what I was reading. Wiesel and other prisoners watched. Some wept. Many were broken. One man yelled out, "Where is God?" Then Wiesel was pushed past the gallows. He writes,

"Behind me, I heard the same man asking: 'Where is God now?' And I heard a voice within me answer him:

'Where is He? Here He is—He is hanging here on this gallows...'"

Two things stirred in me that morning.

First, there was a visceral response to the horror of the story. I felt sick for the boy, and for the victims watching. I even felt something for the perpetrators for what kind of sickness must come over a man that he would follow such an insane order? I became aware of my uncomfortable place in this story. Here I was, some 70 years later, enjoying the warmth of an easy chair and coffee while reading of this nightmare. I felt unworthy to be reading.

Secondly, the terrible beauty of the internal voice Wiesel spoke of was something I recognized. I do not know how Wiesel reconciled all he experienced.

I am unsure of whether he has wrestled with the notion of a suffering Son of God, but instantly, as a follower of the suffering Son of God I knew the voice to be true. In the midst of absurdity there was only one explanation… it was even more absurd.

Where was God? He was hanging on the gallows… with those men… with that young boy. I shuddered. Truly the only thing more haunting than an innocent young boy being murdered in public is the innocent Son of God being murdered in public.

I felt cold.

I thought, "this is a terrible way to start a new year."

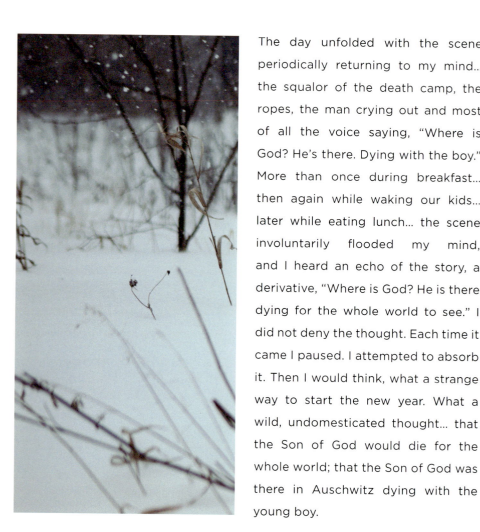

The day unfolded with the scene periodically returning to my mind... the squalor of the death camp, the ropes, the man crying out and most of all the voice saying, "Where is God? He's there. Dying with the boy." More than once during breakfast... then again while waking our kids... later while eating lunch... the scene involuntarily flooded my mind, and I heard an echo of the story, a derivative, "Where is God? He is there dying for the whole world to see." I did not deny the thought. Each time it came I paused. I attempted to absorb it. Then I would think, what a strange way to start the new year. What a wild, undomesticated thought... that the Son of God would die for the whole world; that the Son of God was there in Auschwitz dying with the young boy.

Speaking of undomesticated, I must introduce you to my daughter, Quincy. She lit up the world only after she lit up her father's heart.

I will never forget the first time I met her, which of course, was moments after she arrived. It was this father's first experience at... well, being a father.

Truly something happened to me in our first encounter. I turned from attending to her mom. Quincy's gaze met me half way across the room. Arrested by this energy emanating from her I simply paused. I stared back.

I was sure newborns were unable to focus, but the more she looked at me I was unsure newborns were unable to focus.

Her deep blue eyes blinked in slow motion. It sounded or maybe felt like something snapped deep inside of me. This diminutive, helpless baby girl brought an avalanche.

My heart broke.

I was in love.

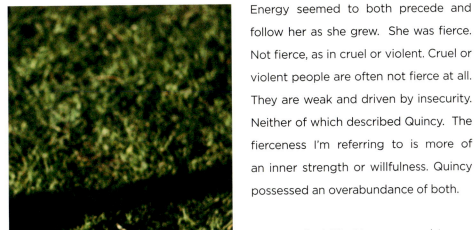

Energy seemed to both precede and follow her as she grew. She was fierce. Not fierce, as in cruel or violent. Cruel or violent people are often not fierce at all. They are weak and driven by insecurity. Neither of which described Quincy. The fierceness I'm referring to is more of an inner strength or willfulness. Quincy possessed an overabundance of both.

She attacked life. Her mom and I were amazed at the energy she unleashed on the world (on our world!). I realized while she was at an early age I had little ability to control her. When she was around the age of two I distinctly remember thinking "Oh man, I cannot tell this little girl what to do." My next thought was, "I am definitely not in control." Slowly it dawned on me, "I must never let her know I know this."

When she was between the ages of 18-36 months, we lived in a small apartment in Arizona. We often left our windows open in the winter, enjoying the breeze of the desert climate.

Quincy stirred up trouble on more than one occasion. She stirred up so much trouble that she grew adept at knowing when parental punishment was coming.

During these pre-punishment moments, she would take off running through our little apartment, yelling, "Help me! Somebody help me!"

Because our windows were up, virtually everyone in our apartment complex could hear her yelling. We would run after her mortified, imagining our neighbors dialing child protection services. I remember chasing her, taking a detour to get the windows closed, and then chasing her again.

This routine happened so often that her mother and I learned to close the windows first before "tipping our hand."

Quincy's fierce energy served her well. She leveraged it to play soccer, to write songs, to help her mom and dad start churches, to hike mountains, to overcome the challenges of Type 1 Diabetes and to live the way she determined to live. I'm not suggesting we didn't guide her. I believe we did though I never sensed I was able to force her to do anything. She possessed a will. She was strong. She would not be controlled. Borrowing from a line I read a long time ago by an author I have forgotten, Quincy was un-editable. She was not something you could change. You could not add, subtract or divide from her. She was best observed. If we did anything right with Quincy, it was our willingness to simply observe.

We allowed her to be herself.

It was refreshing to see as she grew older how little time she wasted managing her image or pretending to be something she was not. She was learning to be who she was.

This is not insignificant. Becoming one's self is a task made massive by self-imposed and predetermined obstacles. Consider only the latter. Our mother, our body, our birthplace, our personality, our DNA is so far out of our control it can easily be assumed life is either a great joke or a great gift. If it is a joke then, of course, none of this matters. If it is a gift, then there must be a giver. And if there is a giver then someone intentionally made us who we are. If someone intentionally made us who we are, then who we are is who we should be. It is enough.

But, we are not conditioned to think this way. We are inclined to think we must become better, or purer, or different. Even religion (especially religion) can mislead us. My own particular tribe within Christianity, for instance, will routinely voice a prayer such as, "God, help us to be like you." God doesn't need us to be like him. It doesn't work anyhow. It doesn't matter how many times the prayer is repeated we will not be like Him.

Unless… we recognize the immense irony: God's Son became like us.

If you want to be like God… be yourself.

The summer before her senior year of high school, Quincy and I were together in California. We discovered kumquats on this trip. Neither of us previously imagined such a fruit.

A kumquat is about the size of a grape. It appears to be a miniature orange, but it's not peeled and eaten like an orange. Rather, a kumquat is to be consumed whole. We received these directions skeptically, but eventually we shrugged our shoulders and ate. The initial taste of a kumquat is bitter, but upon chewing, becomes sweet. The fruit explodes with flavor. The normal progression of facial expressions is… eyebrows curiously furrowing, lips puckering, and then a look of "what have I got myself into", followed by a slow affirmative head nodding, and finally a smile. The entire progression takes only three or four seconds. The key to enjoying the experience is to allow the flavor of one to enhance the flavor of the other. To give up too soon is to agree to a bitter aftertaste. Paradoxically, a kumquat repels and appeals, is bad and good… is both bitter and sweet. You cannot enjoy a kumquat by skipping the bitterness, focusing only on the sweet.

It is not one or the other.
It is both.

Quincy and I experienced all of this that day. In the California sun, we ate. We grinned. We wiped our chins and laughed at life's flavors.

Not long after the sweetness of that trip, Quincy was ready for college. She committed to a small school outside Kansas City to play soccer and study nursing. Late summer of 2012 she headed off to Mid-America Nazarene University.

We were parents like any other. We scratched our heads attempting to figure out how the wind had blown so much time through the pages of our calendars. Quincy packed her first 2.5 years of college with a lot of activities. She played soccer, was a Resident Assistant, studied nursing, represented the school and maybe most formative, spent time in Haiti serving others. Haiti altered the trajectory of her life. She returned with clarity. Nursing would be her platform. Serving would be her purpose.

I recognize there are many different kinds of college experiences. I believe grace can find young people wherever they may choose to attend school. It was obvious, in this case, that Quincy's university was a great fit for her.

She thrived.

The last six weeks of 2014 were exceptionally good for Quincy.

Finals were over. This was a big relief. If you're a college student, you can appreciate the joy of concluding finals.

She participated in weddings on both sides of her family.

She was able to spend quality time with her mother and me.

She talked, laughed and sang with her brothers (they always sang).

She had significant times with college friends.

She enjoyed the Christmas season with both sides of the family.

Although I've been putting it off... now I'm back to New Years Day... back to the thought of God's Son dying on the cross. Soberly, it kept coming back to me,

"God has died."

We likely spent New Years Day, 2015 as many families did... we played games; we watched football, some took a walk around the farm. It was ordinary. I observed Quincy drawing and working on art in the kitchen. More and more of her time in the weeks leading up to the New Year had been invested writing out scripture in interesting ways. She used different fonts and images. It was for her, a form of prayer. It was a centering on ancient and life-giving words. I paused just over her shoulder. She continued working... "Rejoice evermore. Pray without ceasing. In everything give thanks. For this is the will of God in Christ Jesus concerning you." (KJV) We shared no words. When I walked off, I caught her eye. I guess she stole a glance up at her dad to see his response. I was happy to give her a smile and an approving nod.

Rejoice evermore.
PRAY without CEASING
IN EVERYTHING
Give thanks
for THIS is the will of God
Christ Jesus
concerning you.

1 THESSALONIANS 5:16-18

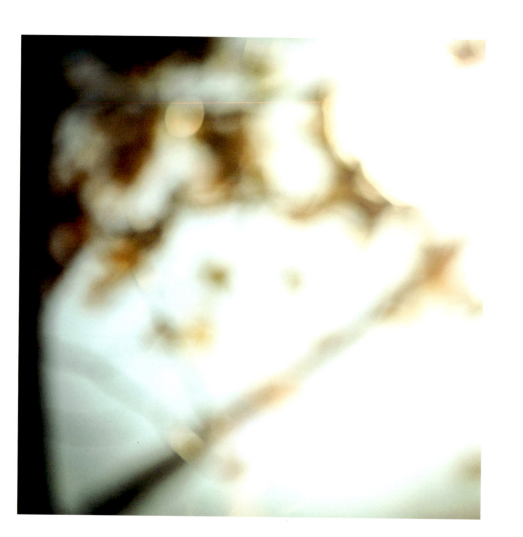

It was Quincy's plan on New Year's Day to travel a couple of hours west of the farm to spend a few days with a friend (yes, a boy!). It was Quincy's first official trip to any boy's family home. She was particularly animated about this relationship. I've heard fathers comment on what it feels like when daughters begin to fall for boys. Usually, the sentiment being expressed is one of loss. For me, I cannot say I felt like I was losing anything. I never thought in those terms. I think in some ways, from the first look in her eye, I knew she was not mine. She was always so much more. Watching her bounce through those last six weeks of the year was fun.

It was a gift... she was a gift.

Meanwhile, Quincy took her time preparing to leave. The delay surprised me until I began to recognize the reason. She was nervous. The thought of the first overnight stay with her friend's family had her slightly flustered.

Finally, she pulled everything together. With her coat on and her backpack over her shoulder, she gave a final hug. I laughed and said, "Are you nervous?" She smiled, blurting, "Yeah! Of course."

Her blue eyes burnished.

In a flash, there was an echo of our first encounter.

The weather didn't appear to be great. It also didn't appear to be worse than a hundred other winter days in Kansas.

Silently, county sized sheets of ice where forming just miles west from where we were.

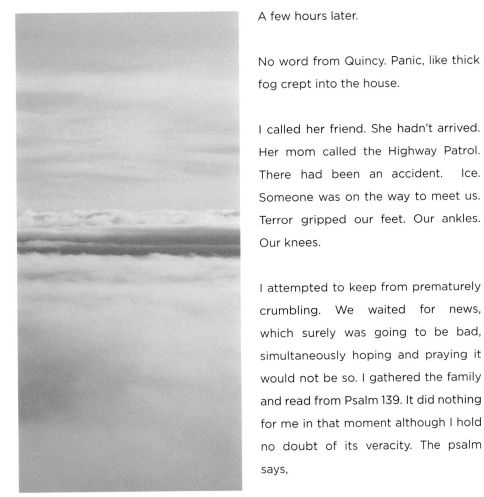

A few hours later.

No word from Quincy. Panic, like thick fog crept into the house.

I called her friend. She hadn't arrived. Her mom called the Highway Patrol. There had been an accident. Ice. Someone was on the way to meet us. Terror gripped our feet. Our ankles. Our knees.

I attempted to keep from prematurely crumbling. We waited for news, which surely was going to be bad, simultaneously hoping and praying it would not be so. I gathered the family and read from Psalm 139. It did nothing for me in that moment although I hold no doubt of its veracity. The psalm says,

Where can I go from your Spirit?

Where can I flee from your presence?

If I go up to the heavens, you are there; if I make my bed in the depths, you are there.

If I rise on the wings of the dawn, if I settle on the far side of the sea, even there your hand will guide me, your right hand will hold me fast.

If I say, "Surely the darkness will hide me and the light become night around me," even the darkness will not be dark to you; the night will shine like the day, for darkness is as light to you. (NIV)

We paced.

We prayed.

Like slamming on the brakes and the gas pedal at the same time, we cried and attempted to stop crying. Finally, from the same front room where my day started, I spotted the headlights. The patrol car made its way from the highway down the gravel road, around the bend, past the barns and up toward the house.

I was so glad to see the patrol car.
I was so scared to see the patrol car.

Once inside, the patrolman bravely dove into a summary of the accident that involved Quincy. Then I observed a slight hesitation and the faintest step backward.

I intuitively recognized he was attempting to create space to give enormous news. There is, of course, simply not enough space for this kind of news.

He did the best he could.

(God bless these men and women who are the ones first to share news such as this.)

He said, "Quincy didn't make it."

Whatever a heartbreaking sounds like… that's what you heard in the room that evening.

It was a thud of darkness. Insanity formed a mosh pit in the middle of my family.

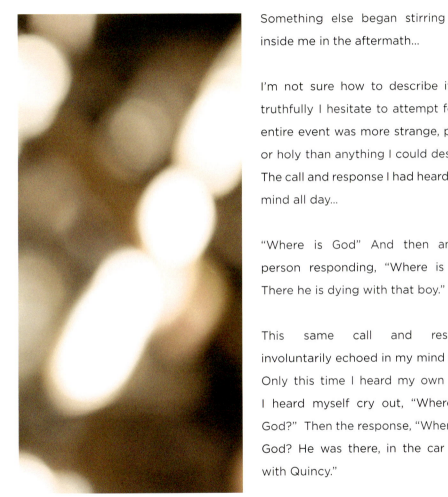

Something else began stirring deep inside me in the aftermath...

I'm not sure how to describe it, and truthfully I hesitate to attempt for the entire event was more strange, painful or holy than anything I could describe. The call and response I had heard in my mind all day...

"Where is God" And then another person responding, "Where is God? There he is dying with that boy."

This same call and response involuntarily echoed in my mind again. Only this time I heard my own voice. I heard myself cry out, "Where was God?" Then the response, "Where was God? He was there, in the car dying with Quincy."

The response gripped me. It was stunning news. To anyone listening in my soul, I whispered, "Maybe it was true. Maybe God was there." I clung to the mystery. It alone kept the darkness at bay.

We packed our suitcases to head home. The bags were heavy; our shoulders heavier. We piled in the car.

Normally five. Now four.

The farm in our rearview mirror, we retraced the route Quincy had just driven. But, our road turned north, skirting the ice, at the eastern edge of the storm.

Our road was then and forever different.

There is, of course, great bitterness here. I have played and replayed the events of that day and the events of her life a thousand times or more.

Like an abandoned rental house full of inconsiderate squatters, the memories come and go in the shelter of my mind. They pay no rent. They are noisy. They offer no solace. They leave little behind except the evidence for their search.

I hear their echoes from time to time, "She was here." "Where is she?" "She's gone!" The voices are shrill. Sometimes my own voice joins them.

The truth is, I am deeply wounded.

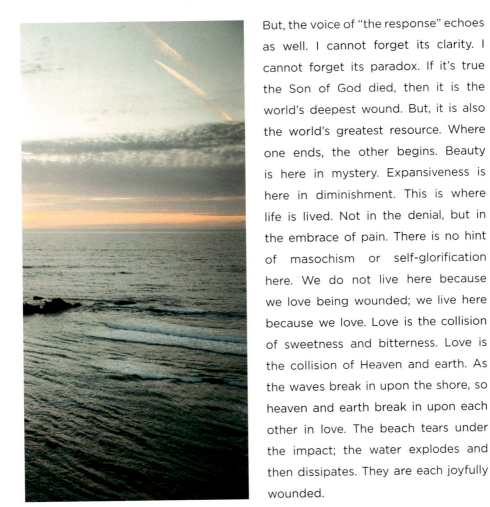

But, the voice of "the response" echoes as well. I cannot forget its clarity. I cannot forget its paradox. If it's true the Son of God died, then it is the world's deepest wound. But, it is also the world's greatest resource. Where one ends, the other begins. Beauty is here in mystery. Expansiveness is here in diminishment. This is where life is lived. Not in the denial, but in the embrace of pain. There is no hint of masochism or self-glorification here. We do not live here because we love being wounded; we live here because we love. Love is the collision of sweetness and bitterness. Love is the collision of Heaven and earth. As the waves break in upon the shore, so heaven and earth break in upon each other in love. The beach tears under the impact; the water explodes and then dissipates. They are each joyfully wounded.

The response I heard that evening was simultaneously the most tragic and beautiful news I have ever heard: My daughter had died… and… God was with her. In the midst of absurdity there was only one explanation… it was even more absurd. In His death, He was present with Quincy in her death.

The same moment she was unable to shake the impact of an oncoming truck, she was also unable to shake the arms of God. He was there. What does this mean? It is an enormous mystery only partially understood…

darkness is Light.
winter is Spring.
bitterness is Sweetness.

Maybe I heard the whisper that holds the world together… joy and sorrow are not mutually exclusive.

Where was God on the worst day of my life?

He was right there.

With my girl.

I wouldn't have wanted Him anywhere else.

Copyright 2015
by Jonathan Foster

ISBN 978-0-692-57703-5

Library of Congress Control Number:
2015919548

Printed in the
United States of America

Design: Matt Johnson, Ruckusgroup.com

Photos: Mark Nagel, Marknagel.com

Wiesel, Elie. Night. New York:Hill and Wang, a division of Farrar, Straus, and Giroux, 1972

Quincy's 1Thess art was almost certainly inspired by the artwork of my new friend,
Breezy Brookshire. Check out The Breezy Tulip Studio at Etsy.com.

1Thessalonians 5:16-18
Scripture quotations marked "KJV" are taken from the Holy Bible, King James Version, Cambridge, 1769. by Biblica, Inc.™ Used by permission. All rights reserved worldwide.

Psalm 139
Scripture quotations marked "NIV" are taken from THE HOLY BIBLE, NEW INTERNATIONAL VERSION®, NIV® Copyright © 1973, 1978, 1984, 2011 by Biblica, Inc.™ Used by permission. All rights reserved worldwide.

To learn more about Jonathan
check out LQVE.org